SALES
ACTUALIZATION
OUTSELLING THE INTERNET

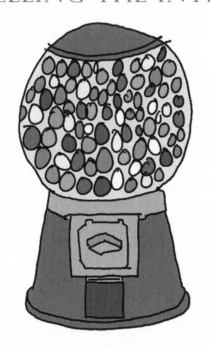

DENNIS O'NEIL
ORIGINAL ARTWORK BY HUGH MACLEOD

To the innovators.

Contents

INTRODUCTION

My face and my voice betrayed my frustration, causing my wife to nudge me. Her mouth silently formed the words, "Be nice!" We had been sitting in a car dealer's showroom for hours, and the long stretches of silence, interrupted only by the sound of shuffling papers, unnerved our whining children who were, understandably, bored out of their skulls.

My wife had selected the car we were buying long before we walked into the showroom. She had spent weeks researching it online, configuring colors as we discussed the options. We saw no need for options and features discussions in the showroom, and the salesperson didn't either. This was a fixed price car. No price haggling, no rebates or discounts, and no negotiations necessary. This should have been a fast and painless experience. But no and no.

Half of our wait was because the finance department wasn't ready, even though we were the only customers in the showroom. We waited in a fog of unknown time, never quite knowing what was happening next or when. Our salesperson got up from his desk frequently, but he never told us what was happening. We assumed there was some progress, but we were confused just enough not to be sure. It was the definition of frustration.

The salesperson had a reasonably straightforward job in front of him, and he added nothing of value to the experience. In fact, he had a negative impact. He asked us very few questions. There was no effort to learn about us, no personal connection, nothing practical. Nevertheless, there he was standing between us and our new car, so we had little choice but to deal with him.

After a while, I wondered if the dealership would be better served by a sales kiosk where we could just order our car. At about the halfway point, I wished a hostess would walk up and hand us one of those discs you get when you leave your name for a table at a restaurant. You know the ones I mean – they blink and vibrate when your table is ready. Maybe the car dealership could do something similar, and it would vibrate when the finance department was ready and again when the car was clean. At least, then, we could take a stroll outside with the kids or something. Alas, no such luck.

These days, unfortunately, this kind of scenario is all too common. Technology and the Internet have brought tools that allow consumers to handle many research and purchase tasks from the comfort of a couch and on their own schedule. As a result, underperforming salespeople have found that the value they used to provide to their customers is increasingly provided by the Internet. This predicament requires salespeople like our car guy to perform at a higher level or risk being replaced completely by a kiosk and a blinky disk.

This is not a new phenomenon. Technology moves fast and has impacted the sales and purchase process since the gumball machine. In the last ten years, however, more than ever before, technology has made serious inroads into some of the core competencies of average salespeople. The Internet has become to sales what robots were to factories in the late 20th century.

So, where does all of this leave today's sales professionals? The successful salespeople of the future will respect technology as both an ally and a challenger. All others will face irrelevance and extinction.

This book is designed to help you avoid extinction and learn how to use technology to your advantage, expanding your sales skills so that a kiosk or a website never make you irrelevant.

CHAPTER 1

THE FIRST LEVEL OF THE SALES ACTUALIZATION PYRAMID

In college, I enthusiastically enrolled in a class titled "Sales & Salesmanship." I had already worked a direct sales position to help pay for school, and I was eager to hear additional perspectives on my newfound professional love. Unfortunately, I sat in class with a furrowed eyebrow, confused about something you'd think would be simple – the definition of a salesperson.

Now, I believe the instructor was a talented salesperson in his own right, and he enjoyed telling us stories about his past sales students more than anything else. He spoke of one student, Todd, with great respect and

transaction facilitation

excitement. Todd worked as a salesperson in the Lawn & Garden department of Sears, and every busy season (spring and summer), Todd sold a tremendous amount of product. He sold so much product, in fact, that he rarely left the cash register.

Hmmm... this is where I started to get confused. If Todd wasn't leaving the cash register, when was he actually ... well, selling?

As the instructor continued his story, what I learned was that Todd had little to no involvement in the purchase decisions for which he received credit. Todd simply managed to be conveniently between the buyers and the store's exit door. By the time those buyers got to Todd, they had already decided what to buy. Todd was not influencing the sale, but merely facilitating the transaction.

THE DIFFERENCE BETWEEN SALES AND SALES SUPPORT

Salespeople, as discussed in this book, make their living selling. Their responsibility is to get the prospect to agree to purchase their product, plus everything that happens before that moment and much of what happens right after. People in sales support, on the other hand, have very different responsibilities.

Salespeople know they've failed when a qualified and well-suited prospect doesn't buy. Sales support staff in the same situation believe it's the product, not them, that has failed. People like Todd, who are in sales support rather than sales itself, don't fail when prospects walk away because they had nothing to do with the

9

decision-making process.

If you're in sales, you already know the difference between sales and sales support. You feel the weight of personal responsibility for all sales activity. On the other hand – with all due respect to the title – few sales associates lose sleep over low sales figures. Dear old Todd is snoozing all through the night, thank you very much.

THE SALESPERSON'S BAD REPUTATION

So, getting back to that definition of salespeople, just what are they? Ask anyone, "What is a salesperson?" and you'll hear a lot of varied responses, many of which won't be so flattering. The more jaded person might describe the sleazy used car salesman stereotype with the plaid jacket and bad hair. Others may have a less specific view, but one thing is for sure – most people don't understand or respect the role of the salesperson.

This disconnect is largely due to the label itself. "Salesman" and "salesperson" have evolved into a cloudy mess of meanings. Thousands of job descriptions involve wearing a name tag or carrying cards with the title of "sales," and these jobs involve a wide range of skills, education, and income. For some consumers, the guy who knocks on your door selling home improvement services is a salesperson. For others, it's the blue shirt people in the TV department. Confusing everyone, people working the cash register in a retail environment are often given the title of "Sales Associate" when they have no more to do with sales than good old Todd.

THE NOBLE GOAL OF SALESPEOPLE

Unfortunately, while sales is rarely viewed by those outside the profession as a noble career choice, successful salespeople often cite a sincere mission as the driving force behind their success. The noble goal of salespeople is to help people make good decisions, and the noble salesperson recognizes that consumers genuinely want help making those good decisions.

After all, the average adult makes thousands of decisions every day. We decide which route to take to work, where to stop for coffee, which grocery store to buy our food, what to eat for lunch, the most effective cold medicine to buy, and on and on. One person can't possibly deeply research each of these decisions without freezing into analysis paralysis.

When making these decisions, we all want advice, reassurance, and justification. This is what the noble salesperson offers, recognizing the value and impact he/she brings to a buying decision. Noble salespeople have a great respect for their influence and wield it to change their clients' lives for the better.

They recognize that lasting and sustainable success comes from remaining significant. They seek to impact the lives of their customers in a positive way, knowing that success will follow as a natural result.

CONSUMERS DON'T CARE ABOUT TECHNIQUE

Consumers care about finding the best products to solve their problems. They don't care about technique or even influence. Nevertheless, it's influence that affects their behavior long after technique has been forgotten. There are techniques for each level of influence we'll explore in this book, but the levels themselves are not achieved sustainably with technique alone.

Zig Ziglar famously said that most people buy on emotion and justify with logic. Well, salespeople sell with influence and execute with technique.

Just like Zig Ziglar's famous statement, the first part of the recipe is an abstract concept, while the second is much more concrete. Technique

15

is a procedure that can be learned. You can perform a technique by doing it. You can only influence by being influential.

Technique is not only valuable, it's invaluable. It's important for a salesperson to know how to learn about a prospect and how to ask them to buy, and there are a number of manuals to teach that. What we're going to explore is a hierarchy of salesmanship based on this more abstract concept of "influence." We're going to discuss what value each of the levels in the hierarchy provides to a buyer and where technology has impacted those expectations.

A HIERARCHY OF BUYER NEEDS

You probably know about Maslow's hierarchy of needs, which details the basis for human growth. It simplifies our needs and describes what we require to sustain growth. Core needs like food and shelter are at the bottom of the pyramid, and more intellectual needs like creativity and spontaneity are at the pinnacle.

The Sales Actualization pyramid is similar. It details the levels of value and influence that a salesperson can yield. The lower levels of the pyramid represent the basic needs of a buyer and the basic skills of a salesperson, while the pinnacle represents ultimate influence.

Todd's job – transaction facilitation – is at the base of the pyramid and is a necessity. A sale cannot complete without it, but it isn't a

17

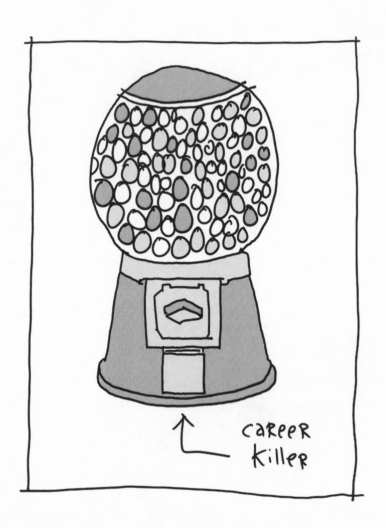

career
killer

18

position of influence. It's the lowest common denominator of sales.

Transaction facilitation is low-hanging fruit for technology. It has been easy to pick off because technology is better at transaction facilitation than humans in almost every way. An early example is the gumball machine. It doesn't miscount change, it works 24/7, and it doesn't give kids dirty looks. It doesn't smile and say "thank you" either, but it does a great job of facilitating transactions. It takes money from a consumer who has already made their purchase decision and returns the product they want without wasting a second of time.

Today, we're way beyond gumball machines. It started with books, but now Amazon.com sells almost every product imaginable. They've grown from just one category to millions of products, and they also facilitate transactions and order fulfillment for other businesses. Amazon.com is the world's best transaction facilitator.

The truth is that consumers don't need salespeople to facilitate transactions anymore. They don't need Todd at the cash register. This doesn't mean that salespeople couldn't or shouldn't facilitate transactions, but it does mean the process is no longer a value differentiator. Simply being in between the product and the exit door is not enough to earn a sale.

As a salesperson, if you're stuck in transaction facilitation, you're in trouble. When you grow as a salesperson and operate at higher levels of the pyramid, your ability to influence a buyer grows exponentially. Each step up the pyramid marks a significant leap in your ability to influence your prospects.

The Internet has steadily climbed the Sales Actualization pyramid, making dramatic strides over the last decade and significantly impacting the buying behavior of consumers. This is why as a salesperson, you need to rise on the pyramid, not just to improve yourself but to stay ahead of the technology that is trying its best to replace you.

CHAPTER 2

INFORMATION ISN'T ENOUGH

Maybe technology can replace salespeople for gumballs, books, and small retail products, but what about technology's role in large purchases? Well, that's a much bigger deal.

Let's say it's 1990, and you need a new car. You see an ad in a magazine or on TV for a model you like, and you want to know the color options. How do you get that information? What about a list of the included and optional features? Dimensions of the trunk? It's 1990, so the only place to get these questions answered is in the dreaded dealership showroom. It wasn't that long ago, but it sounds like the Stone Age from the perspective of 2012, doesn't it?

Sure, you could have called the manufacturer in 1990 and asked them to snail mail you a brochure, but that would have taken time. That simple obstacle gave the salesperson a decided advantage.

Before the Internet, salespeople were the gatekeepers of information. They controlled the data, and you were forced to speak to one of them to get even the most basic answers.

The problem is that in the early stages of considering product options and eliminating the ones that don't measure up, the average consumer isn't ready to speak to a salesperson. It feels unnecessary and uncomfortable when they're just in the "curious" phase of the purchasing process. And if they end up in front of a pushy and intimidating salesperson before they're ready, the situation gets awkward and uncomfortable fast.

Just like Todd stood in between the purchaser and the door at Sears, the car salesperson in 1990 often stood firmly between the prospect and the information they wanted and needed.

A REVOLUTION IN THE 90'S

Then, of course, along came the Internet.
Boom! So, you're interested in buying a car.
What do you do to learn about color options,
features, and trunk dimensions? You go online.
Consumers quickly celebrated the Internet as
their replacement source for data. It's easier,
of course, but there's also an inherent belief by
consumers that salespeople might not give them
the whole story. There's a distrust consideration
that ranges from "This salesperson might be
withholding information" (the lighter side) to
"This salesperson might be lying to me" (the
most egregious side). Whether dishonesty is
actually common is irrelevant. It has happened
enough that consumers are wary.

As I've said, the Internet does information
better. It provides more of it, faster, and more

accurately than a salesperson ever could. It hands you information 24/7 in blunt facts with no withholding. It's available from your favorite couch or in the palm of your hand. Consumers can and do literally get lost in the information available online.

In the face of the big, powerful Internet, what happens to the salespeople who operate on the low level of the pyramid, just disseminating information? They feel threatened, and they should. These salespeople are relying on their access to information as a differentiator, but that's a little like relying on your fax machine in the era of email. Information used to provide them with power and influence over the sale, making them valuable to the consumer. Well, those days are over. Access to information is simply no longer a value-add in the eyes of the consumer.

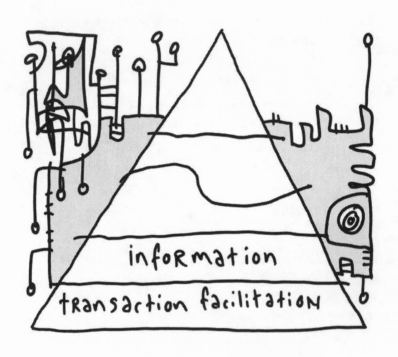

TECHNOLOGY DOESN'T MAKE YOU IRRELEVANT

Yes, it's true that consumer goods like cameras, computers, and mobile phones are researched and compared online to a great extent. The depth of information available to help a consumer make a decision is tremendous – more than any one salesperson could ever know.

In all but a few industries that have closed information circles (like real estate multiple listing services), buyers can get every piece of data they want from the Internet. And those remaining few closed systems of data are being actively and aggressively challenged. Again, technology does it better.

Holding onto the keys to the information gate as a source of power over the consumer is a

27

short-term strategy at best. At worst, it's a sure-fire way for reputation failure when someone disrupts the system.

The death grip on information certainly backfired on car dealerships. Unfortunately, they were arrogant. They had the control and resisted opening the information gates when they could. The salespeople who relied on that information as the source of their power could feel it slipping away with each new subscriber to AOL.

At the same time, the salespeople who sold more than bullet points and numbers were calm. They were selling further up the pyramid, and they knew their influence was much stronger. If you want to experience that kind of calm, you have to sell further up the pyramid, too.

CHAPTER 3

IS TECHNOLOGY AS "WISE" AS THE SALESPERSON?

In the 1990's, the Internet was regularly called the "information superhighway." People would laugh at you if you used that phrase today. In its early days, it was harder for non-users to understand the volume and speed of information that was available via the Internet. Today, we get it, and the volume of online information is staggering even as it continues to grow exponentially.

The web has replaced encyclopedias, dictionaries, and a lot of other research needs that used to send us to the library. Most people today can't imagine doing any research, whether for a purchase or a term paper, without at least starting online.

30

A simple Google search for something like "umbrella store" returns millions of results. The problem then becomes where to start, and this is where the Internet begins to fail. Just because I have lots of information, it doesn't mean the information is helpful (or even accurate a lot of the time). Even if the information has the potential to be helpful, it doesn't mean I know what to do with it or how to apply it.

In other words, holding a hammer doesn't make me a carpenter. And therein lies the opportunity for the salesperson.

DUMP THE FEATURES

"Feature dumping" is a term for that awkward period in the sales presentation when the salesperson, for lack of something better to say, rattles off a list of product features one by one as if the poor customer is going to scream, "YES! I'll take it!"

All salespeople have been guilty of feature dumping at some point in their careers. Like most of your own mistakes, it's easier to spot when you see someone else doing it. And when you do see it, you'll notice the glazed look that appears on the customer's face. The feature list has been memorized by the salesperson, as if the prospect needs someone to recite the brochure out loud.

If you haven't figured this out yet, feature

dumping is discouraged by sales authorities everywhere. The process of speaking feature after feature after feature to a prospect with an expectation that this will influence them to buy is misguided.

Why? Feature dumping is just a list of data – it's information only. It doesn't tell your prospect why they should care or how the features could solve their problems. Feature dumping sort of throws the hammer at your customer without teaching them how to use it.

The Internet is the biggest feature dumper. Ever.

WHEN INFORMATION IS FREE AND UBIQUITOUS, CONSUMERS VALUE PERSPECTIVE

So, the smart salesperson does something more. Instead of just sharing facts, he/she interprets them.

Because the Internet has just feature dumped all over the customer, this person needs help interpreting that data. Consumers crave perspective, and yes, perspective is available on the Internet each day via online magazines, blogs, and review websites that all share opinions and are designed to help consumers

information wants to be free.
perspective wants to be expensive.

make decisions.

But the huge flaw in this source of perspective is that the writers of this online content don't know their reader. Consumers value facts interpreted in a way that solves their problems, not an assumption that their problems are just like everyone else's.

There are at least thousands of digital camera comparison articles available online. Some of them compare just two cameras, while others compare a dozen. The writers do their best to boil down the group to a recommendation of cameras based on the best performing, best value, etc. Except we know that the "best value" for one person is not the same for another. These writers are forced to make generalizations about their readers, so their advice inherently lacks specificity.

The Internet can't possibly know that a camera of a certain size, regardless of its quality, will never work for this buyer because it isn't compatible with this particular person's other equipment. The blog writer can't know that the suggested minivan is unacceptable to a buyer because the seats can't be removed during his annual camping trips.

So, in this arena, salespeople have the

37

advantage. As a salesperson, you can ask questions and find out the needs of your customer. You can also benefit from the buyer's tone of voice, body language, facial expressions, and the people they bring with them. You can find out where your customers live, their goals, and what they're trying to improve or fix. You don't have to generalize to your audience because you have an audience of one that allows you to be laser-specific.

As a result, you can disqualify the incompatible camera and the minivan with fixed seats and still determine the best choice for your customer from the remaining options. This means that you are in a position to help consumers interpret the data in a way that solves their specific problems, not the problems assumed by the writer of a blog.

The Internet is a generalist. Salespeople are highly personalized.

WHAT AM I MISSING?

Consumers don't know what they don't know, and everyone fears the unknown. When a consumer hires an attorney, an accountant, or a doctor, they hire them for their expertise and guidance. An individual may have a general understanding of the court system, but they hire an attorney because they recognize the significance of what they don't know.

These professionals address the questions and concerns their clients bring them, but they also present new things to consider. These experts ask new questions, provide a fresh perspective, and propose new potential solutions. A doctor might recommend a different treatment plan to avoid long-term conflicts with another medication. An accountant might suggest signing a document today to save you from

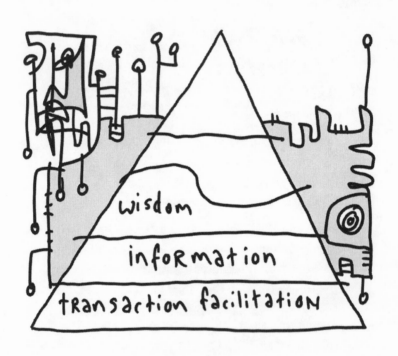

liability ten years from now.

It isn't just about interpreting the data the consumer already has. It's about helping them find the data they didn't even know they were missing and helping them interpret that, too.

Salespeople who demonstrate an ability to solve problems consumers didn't know they were going to have make their customers feel comfortable and confident enough to say "Yes."

This is Wisdom, and it's the next rung on the Sales Actualization pyramid.

Whether explicit or not, this is the most common expectation of a salesperson's role in the buying process today.

Consumers expect more than a cashier and they can get all the feature dumping they need from the Internet. They need solid, personalized Wisdom.

We've all bought something from a less than adequate salesperson. At the end of the process, you're left with an "I could've done that faster by myself" feeling. The salesperson added nothing and actually detracted from the buying experience. This is why we're okay with self-checkout lines at the grocery store and why

I wished for a self-service kiosk in the car dealership.

Today, success in sales requires that you add value to the process or get out of the way, and that's why it's important to cultivate Wisdom in your sales approach.

CHAPTER 4

THE INTERPRETATION OF DATA

My elementary school teachers used to tell me to look in the dictionary when I needed to find the spelling of a word. It didn't make sense to me then, and still doesn't today. Finding the answer when you don't know what you're looking for requires luck or, at the very least, some educated guessing.

This is where the great "worldwide web" trips up again. From a sales perspective, the Internet's Achilles heel is very clear – it has been built on the premise that people know what they're looking for.

Think about all the search boxes you see online. You're expected to know what to type in that box in order to find what you're after. Sometimes, you know what you're looking for, but often, you don't. Or you have an idea of what you want, but you don't know the correct words or phrases to describe it. Even more often, like me as a kid trying to find the spelling of the word in the dictionary, you don't know what you don't know.

CUSTOMERS DON'T KNOW WHAT THEY WANT

That marketing adage, "Give the customer what they want" assumes that the customer already knows what they really want. But an experienced salesperson is aware that even if a customer knows what he/she wants, knowing what will work best for them is another thing altogether.

It isn't that consumers are uneducated. It's the opposite. They've made the best decision based on the data they have. The flaw is in their interpretation of that data. They're unaware of how factor x, y, and z impact the price. And they haven't considered how choice a, b, and c might not work with their lifestyle. They don't know that factor d, e, and f have anything to do with it, or that u, v, and w are even available to them.

45

a thousand points of insight
clustering around a single sale etc.

Henry Ford famously said, "If I asked my customer what they wanted, they would've said a faster horse." Steve Jobs said, "If I asked my customers what they wanted, they would've said a faster typewriter." Henry Ford didn't invent the car, but he made it affordable to many Americans. Steve Jobs didn't invent the MP3 player, the cell phone, or the personal computer, but he made them beautiful and fun to use. We don't always know what we want until someone presents us with the solution.

And the Internet can't do that kind of thing. No, consumers need people for those kinds of discoveries. And they need salespeople to listen to problems, ask questions, and clarify what they're really after. They need salespeople to present the better, often hidden, solutions.

They need salespeople to say, "This is what you want," and they need those salespeople to have asked enough of the right questions to be right with the answer.

BUT WAIT!
DON'T GET
COMFORTABLE

The Wisdom level of the Sales Actualization pyramid is a good place to be, but it's far from a safe stopping point. You see, the Internet is getting smarter, and it's trying to become part of the wisdom business, too.

Since the launch of social tools like Facebook, Twitter, YouTube, and the others like them, people have started to use the Internet differently. The web is slowly transforming from strictly a consumption platform to a publishing platform as well. Our online activities share who we are and who our friends are. We've started clicking [LIKE], [DISLIKE], and [+1] buttons to share our sentiments. We give restaurants 1-5 stars and re-share content we especially love.

We're checking in to local establishments from our phone and leaving comments and tips for the next person.

The Internet is gathering information about the types of movies, music, and writing we like, where we go on the weekends, and where we get our gas.

So, who cares? Well, as a salesperson, you should. This data is harvested and archived in ways that allow it to be analyzed in milliseconds. Consumer sharing and self-expression online has built an elastic personalized database of collective wisdom. The Internet knows what you like and also what your friends like.

Does this make the Internet as wise as a salesperson? Not yet and not in every way, of course, but in some ways, it's already wiser. As the amount consumers share online increases, the recommendation engines of the future will be better equipped and possibly more accurate and efficient than a salesperson. Ouch!

What makes the collective wisdom of the Internet most powerful is that this data is being collected with context – examining how we are all connected to one another. It knows other people like you, it knows who influences you, and it knows about your relationships. This means the Internet is taking two steps up the pyramid in one leap, and it means you have to stay a step – or two – ahead of it.

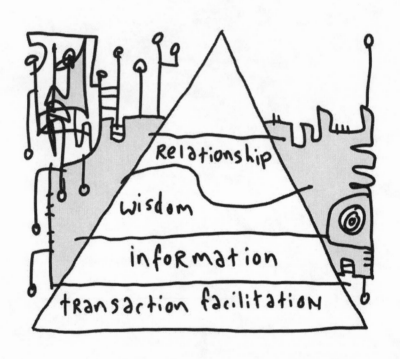

CHAPTER 5

THE GAME OF RELATIONSHIPS IS CHANGING

Rightfully so, consumers recognize that salespeople aren't impartial, so trust is an uphill battle for the salesperson. We want to sell customers our products, but it's our responsibility to demonstrate that our impartiality doesn't equal dishonesty. It's perfectly acceptable to have a very clear opinion (i.e., that people should buy your product), but it's hardly noble to lie in order to convince people of that.

It's always the salesperson's responsibility to earn trust and respect, and it's the consumer's prerogative to give or take trust and respect. Some consumers will offer it until you prove you don't deserve it, but the opposite is more often true. As a salesperson, you start at less than zero on the trust scale.

But if you're already a customer's friend, that's different. You've established at least a minimal level of trust, so you get a "trust head start." You don't start below the zero line like a salesperson who is a stranger.

If a customer maintains a positive opinion of you as a friend or acquaintance, you get a big head start and a significant trust advantage. Friends are given an advance because of the relationship.

This is why Relationship stands just above Wisdom on the Sales Actualization pyramid. This level is a transitional level in which we don't just sell to customers, but we begin to see them buying from us.

Staying well-connected with customers and potential customers has long been a tool of successful salespeople. Relationships help establish both rapport and opportunity – two elements that can close a sale.

RAPPORT AND OPPORTUNITY

It's a lot easier to establish rapport when you have an existing relationship. Building rapport takes time, even for the salespeople with the best people skills. In turn, relationships benefit from existing rapport. Relationships leverage familiarity, accelerate the sales process, and amplify influence.

As for opportunity, relationships bring salespeople top-of-mind when their connections or friends need their services. As a consumer, if you need a product or service, it's appealing to have a friend or acquaintance with access to it.

The relationship provides your buyer with a feeling of comfort and trust that the advice they receive from you is honest. This also makes getting to a decision easier.

Instead of expending the effort searching for the right salesperson, relationships can win a sale simply because the familiar salesperson represents the shortest distance to a resolution.

WHO DO YOU TRUST?

People don't always trust their friends, but they know which friends to trust. I know which of my friends are smart, for example, and which of them are full of it. I know which friends I can count on if I need a kidney and which friends I couldn't count on for bus fare. Friendship does not automatically create trust.

Trust has a contextual component, too. I know my friends' respective areas of expertise, and I know on what subjects they're clueless. In other words, I know if and when their advice will be valuable to me.

If my friend thinks that the McRib is the best sandwich ever, I'm not going to ask him for fine dining suggestions. I won't ask my uncoordinated friend for tennis lessons or my single friends for marriage advice. This doesn't mean their input has no value, but their advice will be weighted by my perception of their expertise.

Trust, as it relates to influence, cannot be defined by a person alone. It involves both the person and the subject matter at hand.

AN OPENING TOOL

When consumers look for recommendations online for anything from movies and music to cars, school systems, or coffee, they value the recommendations from familiar sources over those of strangers. When in this consideration phase of a purchase, asking hundreds or thousands of their friends for advice can be just a few keystrokes away.

It stands to reason then that a salesperson's best opportunity to be a part of this consideration process is to be one of those connections. This is why relationships that begin before the sale are more valuable than relationships that grow during and after the sale. A salesperson with an existing connection to a consumer who seeks advice has automatically earned an opportunity to win the sale.

So, you can build a relationship with a consumer

before the need for the product or service arises. You're still a salesperson, but you were connected before the need to buy. This means that there is, at minimum, a small level of familiarity and trust already established, and your chances of influencing the purchase have increased dramatically.

Of course, a relationship may not be enough to get the sale. Most of us try to buy from friends when we can, but we will buy elsewhere if it means a substantially bigger benefit. Still, the relationship definitely gives you, as a salesperson, a better opportunity to make the sale.

RELATIONSHIPS AND THE INTERNET

How does technology affect salesperson-consumer relationships? As is often the case, it makes relationships both easier and more competitive for salespeople.

Besides the ability to survey our friends online about a product or business, we can also proactively warn our connections of bad businesses. We can blog about a bad experience at the oil change shop or share the story of our awful meal at a local restaurant.

But if you're a consumer, and you want to find out a friend's experience of a product or business, will your friends be listening and available when you ask? With an average number of connections online, all but the most obscure questions will get some response within 24 hours. But what if you want an answer now? The Internet has obliterated our patience levels.

Can we do better? Yes.

We know that online social tools enable us to collectively harness the wisdom of our connections, as well as our connections' connections. Everyone shares information, but not everyone shares it at a convenient time for others to see it when it's relevant to them.

Our online sharing, along with positive or negative sentiments, are being collected in a way that powers how the Internet responds to us, however. We don't have to actively or directly ask our friends because the Internet has begun to do that for us. Instead of asking for dinner recommendations on Facebook and waiting for responses, the Internet knows our friends' recommendations if they've already shared their opinions. Maybe we weren't online when they shared it the first time, or we forgot about seeing it in the past. But the Internet didn't forget. It saved the opinion and can share it with us now that we're asking.

The Internet can access more than our circle of friends, too. It can use anonymous and non-anonymous data from our friends' friends. No, you don't know these people, but most of us will take the recommendation of a friends' friend before the opinion of a stranger.

Of course, there are exceptions. You don't want to be influenced by your deadbeat cousin's friends. But if you respect someone, you might be willing to be influenced by the opinions of that person's friends. Wouldn't it be worth having their insight and maybe even the sentiments of their connections to answer your questions?

THE RECOMMENDATION ENGINE

So, what's the real value of a recommendation engine? If I'm shopping Amazon.com and considering a book purchase, I'm presented with user reviews of that book. With popular books, there are sometimes thousands of reviews. Clearly, I'm not going to read them all, and Amazon does a lot to drive the most influential reviews to the top by asking people for a click if a review was helpful.

It would be better for me as a customer, though, if I knew the people who left the reviews. Using the social recommendation engine:

• Amazon product reviews would be sorted, or at least highlighted, with reviews by my Facebook friends, LinkedIn connections, or people I follow on Twitter.

• A second level would be available that would highlight my Facebook friends' friends, and my "seconds" on LinkedIn. Maybe no one I know personally has read a book I want to know about, but my friend Cassandra's boss says it's worth a read. Sold!

Shopping for a home online is especially overwhelming, what with bedrooms, bathrooms, square footage, property taxes, blah, blah, blah. None of this information tells me what it's like to live in the home or the neighborhood. None of it is very helpful in answering the questions I don't know to ask.

So, future real estate recommendation engines will be powered by social data. We'll research a home based on how it blends with our own social data and the data from our friends.

• When we research an address, we'll learn that our friend jogs past the home once a week because she shares her fitness routines online.

• We'll learn that our high school friend checks in at the coffee house around the corner and warns us to stay away from the muffins after 3pm.

• We'll see that a co-worker reviewed a nearby

diner and gave it 5 stars on Yelp.

● We'll learn that three of the bands playing on our favorite Pandora station are scheduled to play at nearby venues in the next few months.

These things tell me what kind of life I would experience while living in that house. The bottom line is that data doesn't sell; feelings do.

SCHEDULED SERENDIPITY AND UNSOLICITED ADVICE

You aren't building a relationship with the Internet itself, of course, but it will use your relationships to learn about you. The Internet of the near future will likely be a place where we receive lots of unsolicited advice.

We may be shopping for a book and be told that our friends would recommend a different choice. We may check-in to a restaurant and be told what appetizer we're going to love. You know that one friend who knows you so well that she always gets you the best birthday presents? Her new name is the Internet.

What we think of as the "search box" is

changing. Soon, that search box may come back with an unexpected response like, "No. I know what you asked for, but this is what you really want." And it might be right.

When it comes to sales, this is a relationship game-changer.

CHAPTER 6

LOGIC VS. MEANING

With all of these rapid advances in technology, how does the salesperson stay relevant? Where should successful salespeople focus their growth efforts, and what types of salespeople will be successful in the future?

As we've already established, the bottom two levels of the Sales Actualization pyramid – Transaction Facilitation and Information – have been sufficiently taken over by the Internet. These jobs are no longer done by salespeople, or at least they no longer need to be done by salespeople.

These duties are either 100% electronic, or the tasks are done by non-sales clerks who make an hourly wage. The clerks are sometimes given the title of "Sales Associate," but the expectations for

SALes:

x: money
y: pRoduct
z: a vast
    JUNGLe
of psychological
   VARiables...

their actual sales abilities are pretty low.

The Wisdom and Relationship levels of the Sales Actualization pyramid are strong levels for salespeople to operate within. Yes, the Internet is undoubtedly encroaching into this territory and these skill sets, but its abilities are still weaker than what consumers want ... at least for now. There's no telling exactly when the Internet will evolve into a serious threat to these skill differentiators, but it will likely happen faster than we'd like to think.

DON'T RELY ON LOGIC ALONE

A common theme that begins at the Relationship level and extends upward is: Building a connection to the consumer that transcends the exchange of money.

Salespeople operating on higher levels of the pyramid create a purchase environment, not where money is no object, but where it isn't the only object and definitely not the main object.

When your relationship with your consumer is based solely on the purchase and exchange of money, you have only a single, very thin, and very logical thread that connects you with the consumer. It's so thin, in fact, that it only takes one new variable – a competitor with a cheaper price, a new option, or even one small mistake on your part – to break the thread forever.

As a salesperson, you need something stronger and, yes, something illogical. You don't want people to make illogical decisions, but you also know that decisions are not made with logic alone. How a decision makes a customer feel is just as important as how it affects the wallet.

In order to create multiple threads, you need a connection that will not be substantially impacted by a similar product that's offered for less. A competitor can always be a few pennies less, but if you have multiple strings connecting you to your customer, you can weather a storm. You can take a hit from a competitor. You can make a mistake. You can absorb these hits and still have the opportunity to maintain your business. Even if one sale doesn't go your way, your connection with that customer will bring you another opportunity.

The salesperson who only speaks to their clients when they're spending money are the easiest ones to leave. There's no bond beyond the sale, nothing beyond the money. That's a thin, easily breakable thread for sure.

ESTABLISHING MEANING

The pinnacle of the Sales Actualization pyramid is Meaning. Beyond Information, Wisdom, and Relationships, we buy from people or brands who mean something to us.

Apple Computer is a great example because it's seen as a bulletproof brand that connects with many consumers who identify themselves as cool, creative, and tech savvy. This brand personality permeates everything Apple does in the marketplace. It's part of their products, retail stores, and website, and it oozes from every inch and pixel of their marketing. Apple products are much more expensive than their competitors, and their hardware specifications are rarely equal to the competition. Many have argued that their specs are poor when price comparisons are made, but this doesn't matter to the typical

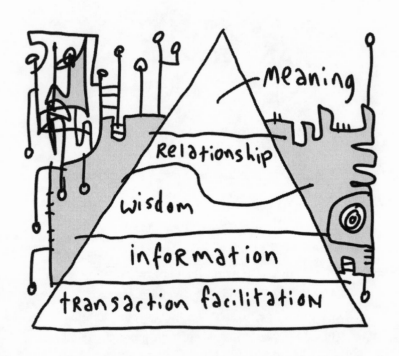

Apple customer. Yes, people buy Apple products because they perform beautifully, but many Apple customers buy because Apple's brand reflects who they are or want to be. They are Apple customers.

Consider what it might be like for a typical Apple customer to buy a Zune. Don't know what a Zune is? Me either, but I've been told that Microsoft used to make an MP3 player (you know, an iPod), and they called it a Zune. A typical Apple customer would be embarrassed to be seen with a Zune. It simply isn't "who" they are.

These customers don't consider an option B. There is no option B to them. They identify with the Apple brand to a level that surpasses the power of all the other levels of the pyramid. It means something to them to be an Apple user, so they are. Using something else would require a fundamental change in how they see themselves ... or a denial of how they see themselves. Who wants to do that?

THE OPPORTUNITY
FOR SALESPEOPLE

If you look at this level of magnetism created by
Apple and other companies, it's easy to think
it's all about marketing. After all, the marketing
department created the brand persona, didn't
it? If so, we just have to hope that our own
marketing departments know what they're
doing.

Creating a broad brand identity usually
requires a significant amount of content and
can cost millions of dollars between television
commercials, billboards, online content,
magazine ads, and more. But the truth is that
as a single salesperson, you don't need your
identity to reach as broad an audience as a
brand like Apple. You only need your identity
to provide enough business for you. Plus,
creating content or media has never been easier

or less expensive for the individual. Sure, the Internet may be eating away at the less skilled salesperson's job security, but at the same time, it's empowering the savvy salesperson who is willing to grow to reach new buyers by taking advantage of these new tools.

Marketing departments define what it means to own the product. Great salespeople define what it means to be their customer. This is meaning, and it's the ultimate differentiator.

ONE OF A KIND

In your battle against commoditization and obsolescence, the single differentiator you have as a salesperson is that you are unique. Nearly all of the marketing books out there preach the value of attaching an attractive persona to your business – one that appeals to consumers.

If/when you are a salesperson at the peak of your skill level, you create this same inbound commitment from your buyers. You communicate not only what makes your product or service unique, but what makes buying from you unique. You define for your prospects what it means to be your customer.

Every customer is different, and so is every salesperson. No two salespeople show up for work for the same reasons each day. No two salespeople pick up the phone with the same thought. Salespeople show up every day realizing their own goals and solving their own problems, just like consumers. These identifiers are unique, and they're our last true differentiator as salespeople. As long as you choose to show what makes you different, it will be clear to your buyer that there is no other salesperson like you.

Your job is to demonstrate not only what makes you unique, but what it means to do business with you. Here are some potential reasons someone might buy from you:

- You support the same charity as your customer.

- Your children are the same age as your customer's.

- Your customer's family buys from you

- You and your customer have a similar sense of humor.

- You and your customer are both fans of the same sports team.

- You and your customer are members of the same church.

- You and your customer are active in the same political party.

- You make your customer feel good about themselves.

Sometimes, a customer might even buy from a salesperson who appears to need help. Have you ever gone to a store and bought something from the "trainee" who totally bungled their presentation? The presentation was so bad you had to help them find the answers you were looking for? You bought from them not because they were a great salesperson, but because you respected their efforts and understood what it's like to be green on a job. Obviously, that isn't a recommended tactic, but consumers want to buy from someone who provides additional meaning to the transaction ... even though they don't have to. The salespeople who achieve a meaningful connection secure an unmatched level of permanence in the minds of their buyers.

Sure, a buyer can change, and the salespeople they identify with can also change as a result. But if you, as a salesperson, successfully demonstrate what it means to buy from you, then you make yourself irreplaceable and not duplicable. When you make that kind of connection, the buyer doesn't consider it an option to buy from any other salesperson. Just as a loyal Apple customer feels, buying from someone other than you would go against who your buyer is as a person. They buy from you.

Someone else might offer a little better value,

but no one can be you. No Internet and no other salesperson – except someone they begin to identify with more – can compete with that. And that's the power of the ultimate differentiator – meaning.

CHAPTER 7

DEEP SELLING

How can you operate at the Meaning level?
Similar to the Relationship level, the Meaning
level of Sales Actualization has more to do with
intent than technique.

Learning techniques alone is insufficient because
a technique can only be effectively applied in an
exact scenario. Selling, relationships, people,
and emotions are hardly exact scenarios. You
can't memorize sales techniques to handle
every situation. You can learn what to say if the
customer says this or that, but what happens
when they say something you haven't prepared
for.

Once you understand what it means to do
business with you and can communicate that
to your customer, you can handle any sales
situation without the need for memorization.

SHOW, AND THEY TELL

People who are honest don't walk around professing their honesty. People who are truly hard workers don't spend the work day telling everyone how hard they work. If a salesperson greeted you with, "Hi, I'm Sally, and I'm an honest salesperson," you're likely to laugh or back away slowly.

Yet, companies end up doing this same thing in their marketing messages. People have become deaf to tag lines like "Integrity, Honesty, and Value." Words are cheap; prove it.

Showing people what you believe is infinitely more powerful than telling them. This has always been an advantage for salespeople. Instead of relying on marketing messages alone, you can demonstrate to clients face to face who you are.

Advantage: Salespeople.

ALL REAL CONVERSATIONS ARE CUSTOM-MADE

If there's a new tool that has been identified as the savior of all problems in business, it's social media. The ability to converse both directly and publicly with anyone anywhere provides major opportunities for building connections. It also provides the lazy with plenty of opportunities to spam masses of people with generic, poorly timed marketing messages.

Real conversation is critical to relationship building, which means relationships can't be automated. There's no such thing as an automated conversation. No one feels a connection to the automated voice on the telephone just because it responds to your answers.

Relationships are created one-on-one, and you start from zero every time. Tomorrow's customer will not give you the benefit of the relationship that you formed with today's customer.

Unlike the spam or the automated voice, actual effort is required to have real conversations. They're "custom-made." So, if you memorize, you may as well use an automated voice.

LEAVE THE STAGE

Most advertising and sales presentations are designed to speak at someone, as if on a stage. It's a non-level position. The concept of a sales presentation is, "I talk. You listen." This is great for the salesperson's ego. Salespeople who do this get to be a star, hearing the wonderful sound of their own voice showing off just how knowledgeable they are.

I'm sure you know salespeople, or people who aren't even in sales, who never leave the stage. No matter how hard you try to connect with them, you always feel like they're performing for you. They're always "on," and you wish they'd come down off the stage for just a moment to have a real conversation with you.

There are two main problems with staying "on stage." First, a lot of what salespeople do "on stage" is share information. We have already learned that knowledge (information) is a commodity and holds little value and credibility when coming from a salesperson. Second, it isn't possible to develop a real relationship with someone who isn't truly open. Staying on stage means you keep a distance between yourself and the buyer.

The stage doesn't work well for consumers. If they're going to benefit from your wisdom and have any chance at developing a relationship with you that holds meaning for them, you need to have a peer-to-peer, same-level conversation.

NOT EVERYONE IS YOUR BUYER

Many sales authorities have worked hard to teach salespeople that every prospect entering their office is their buyer. Unfortunately, this just isn't true. Management prefers not to consider this point of view because yield-inclined salespeople use the "they're just not my buyer" excuse to provide shelter from true accountability.

But the truth is not everyone can be your buyer. You must define what it means to own your product, and to define this, you have to recognize that there will be some people it won't fit.

Selling is not the process of showing product after product to someone until they say "yes." That's brokering. Selling is the process of matching the prospect to the product you have,

and the reality is that sometimes, there will be
no match.

This doesn't mean that you shouldn't be working
your hardest at making the sale. Before you give
up, make sure a prospect has proven they're
not your buyer. Sell from a position of strength.
You're the gateway to a valuable product
that could potentially change the life of your
prospect. While they don't need to prove to you
that they're worthy, they do need to be a match
for it.

DEEPLY SOLD

Selling is sharing the power of your product
in such a way that builds a desire inside the
prospect. You make it fit so perfectly into their
lives, painting a path that shows how your
product is a clear, simple, and beneficial solution
to their problems. The buyer makes the decision
to buy.

When a prospect is deeply sold in this way, they
make the decision for themselves, and asking
for the sale becomes a mere formality. For the
deeply sold prospect, not buying would involve a
sense of loss.

It isn't possible to be deeply sold on something
that's forced upon you. People rarely want things
that are pushed on them. There's no need.

A deeply sold customer will take the product
from your hands.

CHAPTER 8

THE SELF-RELIANT SALESPERSON

Generally speaking, the responsibility of marketing is to bring people in the door, and the responsibility of salespeople is to close the deal. The modern purchase process, however, is anything but general, predictable, or perfect.

From a salesperson's point of view, having a marketing department that delivers a steady stream of qualified prospects is the ideal scenario. Nevertheless, it doesn't do anything for your security as a salesperson. If the marketing department fails, has its budget slashed, or is eliminated altogether, that steady supply of qualified prospects is gone, and your livelihood is gone with it.

Relying solely on the marketing department doesn't do anything to build your individual

value in the eyes of the consumer either. In order
to build a lasting business, you'll seek to control
your own success by building deep relationships
with your clients and establishing your own
identity (aligned with your product, of course).

The best salespeople, in fact, succeed in spite
of their market. Their volume doesn't swing
radically with market fluctuations because
they're in charge of their prospect stream
and don't allow their sales opportunities to
be exclusively controlled by the marketing
department.

While the marketing department has a role
– sometimes, a significant one – the best
salespeople recognize that they are more
successful when they augment the marketing
department's efforts or vice versa. The more
business you build for yourself, the more
business you keep for yourself.

THE LAST MILE

In the early days of broadband Internet, it was a fairly simple process to bring fast data speeds into the local telecom company switches. These are the offices or little buildings in any zip code that act as the hub for telephone and cable distribution.

The technological challenge came in getting those speeds from the telecom offices into homes and businesses. The variables of line quality, cable material, and the actual distance from the home or business to the switch played a role in the challenge. Getting the product to travel the so-called "last mile" and reach its destination was the most difficult, but that was also where the value resided. If they couldn't get the speed to go that last mile, they didn't have a product.

At its core, being a salesperson means handling that last mile. Sales is securing the "Yes" – the customer's agreement to purchase. Sales without the last mile is not sales.

NO LEVEL IS A SUBSTITUTE FOR THE OTHER

The Sales Actualization pyramid is a hierarchy, and to operate at a high level on the pyramid, the levels below it must be functional to be successful. Again, your responsibility is the entire sales cycle. For example, operating at the Relationship level but failing to provide adequate information is a recipe for failure. Imagine having loyal customers show up to your store ready to buy, but not being able to facilitate transactions. That wouldn't work very well, would it?

Nevertheless, if you're operating at the Relationship and Meaning levels of the pyramid, prospective customers will be more forgiving toward you when something goes wrong farther down the pyramid. But just don't forget that each level carries an expectation that the levels below it are being or have been taken care of.

THE SOCIAL MEDIA SWEET SPOT

Awareness -> Trust/Rapport -> Close

A simplified flowchart of the sales process would look something like the above. A consumer has to be aware that your product exists before anything else can happen. The brand, business, or salesperson must establish sufficient trust or rapport. Then, the "Yes" must occur.

Awareness is often considered the domain of the marketing department, while the last – closing the sale – is considered the domain of the sales department. The trust/rapport segment is securely cemented in both camps and is often the longest part of the sales process.

Consider the sales cycle when a prospect enters a retail environment. They showed up, so they're obviously already aware of the business. Asking for the sale only takes a moment. It's everything that happens in between that takes the majority of your time as a salesperson, and it's this segment of the sales process in which social media has the most significant opportunity to scale your efforts. It's the social media sweet spot.

Kaine Homes, a home builder in Maryland, has long been a user of video on their website and in social media. They have video messages from their owner, their sales team, and their administrators available nearly anywhere you find them online. Instead of photography on their "About Us" page, each one of their team members has a short video that describes what they do as a part of the Kaine Homes family.

How does this affect the sales process? When prospects walk into a Kaine model home, they instantly recognize the person greeting them. It's very common to hear a prospect say, "Oh, hey! You're in that video!" There's an instant smile and instant connection.

When a video, a blog post, or even a tweet demonstrates who you are, and shows your personality, readers and watchers will begin to feel they know you. This is why people think they know celebrities. We see them interviewed on television, we watch their movements and behavior on the screen, and we hear the emotions in their voices. It feels like they're talking to us even though we know they aren't, and as a result, it feels like we know them. This gives celebrities an advantage in social situations, and it can give you an advantage as a salesperson, too.

Salespeople who've made themselves available to the public online benefit from a level of familiarity before the prospect enters the door. Kaine Homes' prospects feel comfortable as soon as they see the familiar face in the office. This provides a head start and dramatically increases the speed of the rapport/trust building phase of the sales cycle.

This is another way in which technology becomes your friend and helps you, in turn, develop relationships with your prospects, becoming a more self-reliant salesperson who is not at the mercy of the marketing department.

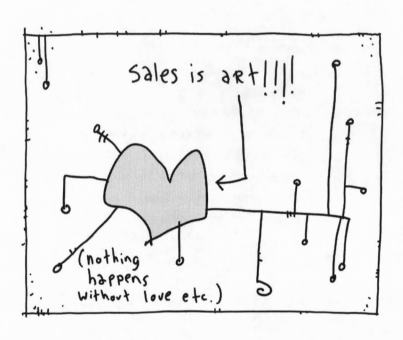

CHAPTER 9

THE ART OF SALES

You might remember a public television show that used to be on the air called The Joy of Painting with Bob Ross. A talented painter, Bob spent 20 minutes during each show walking the audience through everything he did to create a beautiful landscape painting. He talked about which brushes to use, which colors, what areas on the canvas to paint, etc. He described the whole process as he did it right in front of the camera, but as you watched him paint, the experience never quite lined up. He made art look like a trick.

Bob Ross was definitely painting right in front of your eyes, but it was easy to see that you needed much more than the procedure he described to produce a painting as beautiful as his. Procedure alone couldn't help you to be a painter.

Sales is more than a procedure, too. It's an art. The fact that no one can precisely describe what makes a salesperson talented is one way we know it's an art form. You can describe traits of a talented salesperson (empathy, curiosity, boldness), but people can have those traits and not be talented or successful salespeople.

Many consumers would agree that good qualities for a salesperson include labels like "genuine," "authentic," and "intuitive." If you ask a consumer or salesperson how to be genuine, though, it's virtually impossible to put it into words, isn't it? To answer the question, people usually resort to a list of synonyms for "genuine," but they still stop short of describing the action of being genuine. The alternative method is to use a story example that starts something like, "Being genuine is when you..."

It's indescribable. And that's because salespeople are artists of change.

THE SALESPERSON'S IMPACT

Things that develop meaning – art, books, films, paintings, leaders, and yes, salespeople – convert emotions to language and language to emotions. They do one of two things: (1) verbalize what we feel and have not been able to say, or (2) say things that make us feel.

Salespeople are trusted each day to take what the consumer feels and process it into language the consumer can compute or into language the consumer can identify as accurate. Salespeople use language to provide buyers with a solution that connects emotionally to what they need. That creates change, and sales is change.

So, don't minimize your impact on your buyers' lives. Their lives are impacted by seemingly mundane products for many years after they buy. They spend two hours a day commuting in the car you sold them. They'll vacuum their new puppy's dog hair with the vacuum they bought from you for years while that puppy grows into an adult pet. That pillow will make all the difference the night before their big job interview. As a salesperson, you impact life.

If you feel your product makes an insignificant impact on your buyers' lives, rethink how you see that impact, or find a new product.

Influence in the hand of a noble salesperson is a force for good. Unused, it's a wasted opportunity to positively affect the life of your customer. And a salesperson is a terrible thing to waste.

TECHNOLOGY IS MERELY A MEANS TO A GOAL

A salesperson's primary focus is always communication – communicating their product's value and their own value to prospects. Technology creates new ways to communicate, but your focus is your message, not the technological vehicle that carries it.

Technology is certain to evolve, which means the tools you use as a salesperson will change. What won't change are the conversations you have with your prospects and the meaningful relationships you develop.

Technology will continue creeping into the realm of mediocre sales performance, while consumer expectations evolve as well. We're likely to see higher standards for product quality, higher expectations for purchase and ownership experience, and higher expectations for customer service.

PRACTICAL PASSION

Traditional artists – painters, sculptors, musicians, etc. – have a passion for their craft. What is the "craft" of sales? It is the craft of bridge-building; connecting buyers with solutions. The craft alone doesn't directly produce a product. The art is facilitating the process where people make decisions that will make them happier.

There's a reason there are so many "starving artists" in the world. Many have a great passion for their work, but they're rarely adept at helping buyers find their work or understanding what the artistic product could mean to those buyers.

It's great to have a passion for your craft, but if you want a sustainable business, you need to have a passion for what your craft can do for others. And when that happens, you win,

because living that passion will help you stay at
the pinnacle of the Sales Actualization pyramid.

You'll get to keep playing for as long as you want,
no matter the changes that technology brings.
After all, no matter how efficient technology
becomes, it will never be an artist. Only the
salesperson can be that.

ABOUT THE AUTHOR

Dennis O'Neil has been a student of the sale since 1994. Having personally experienced the evolution of the consumer-salesperson relationship alongside the expansion of the Internet, Dennis has long been fascinated by both its impact on how consumers buy and on the steady extinction of the salespeople who refuse to adapt and embrace this change. When not pondering sales theory and practicing its influence, Dennis can be found running a web development and web applications firm outside Baltimore, Maryland, or enjoying the company of his wife and two children.

You can read more from Dennis on his blog:
www.dennisoneil.com

You can follow Dennis on Twitter:
@dennisoneil